© **Telos Art Publishing 2001**

Authors: Hattie Gordon, Tim Porges,
Elizabeth Smith, Anne Wilson, Tina Yapelli
Series Editor: Matthew Koumis
Proof Reader: Vivien Brett
Designed by celsius°
Reprographics by Studio Technology, Leeds
Printed in Italy

Telos Art Publishing
PO Box 125, Winchester SO23 7UJ, England
telephone: +44 (0) 1962 864546
facsimile: +44 (0) 1962 864727
e-mail: editorial@telos.net
www.arttextiles.com

ISBN 1 902015 223

A CIP catalogue record for this book is available
from The British Library

Notes: all dimensions are shown in metric and
imperial, height x width (x depth).

Photo Credits:

Angela Forster, James Isberner, Stephen Pitkin,
Tim Thayer, Mary Jo Toles.

Artist's Acknowledgements

My sincere appreciation to Lucas Cowan, Nancy
Gildart, Mina Heshmatpour, Alan Koeninger,
Charlene Nemec-Kessel, Denise Schober, Cat
Solen, Jenni Sorkin, Laura Ventresca Montgomery,
and Maiko Yamauchi for their friendship and
assistance in the studio. Special thanks to my
husband, Michael Nagelbach, and my family,
whose ongoing belief in my work has been
invaluable.

Hair Work, *Grafts (#2)*, *Devour*, and *Feast* are in
the collection of the Museum of Contemporary
Art, Chicago. *Hair Work* and *Grafts (#2)* are the
restricted gifts of Betty L. Cleeland in memory of
Raymond T. Cleeland. *Devour* is the gift of Ruth P.
Horwich. *Feast* is the restricted gift of Mrs Gerald
S. Wilson, David and Mary Winton Green, Betty L.
Cleeland, anonymous donor, Cleve Carney and
Kay Schmitt, Linda and Tom Dolack, John and
Robyn Horn, Mary K O'Shaugnessy, Gordon and
Claire Prussian, Lynde B. Uihlein, Manfred Muller,
Karen Johnson Boyd, Douglas Dawson and
Wallace Bowling, John and Laura Fraser, Joan
Livingstone, Leah and Jack Bowman, Bonnie Ward
Klehr, Nancy and Harry Koenigsberg, Nina Bliese,
the Artist, and Roy Boyd Gallery. *Found* is in the
collection of the Art Institute of Chicago, Nicole
Williams Contemporary Textile Fund.

Portfolio Collection
Anne Wilson

Natural Orders, no. 3 (detail)
1987–88

Contents

Devour (detail)
1993

left:
Natural Orders, no. 1
1987–8
Fiber, paint
1 x 1m (40 x 40in)

Biography

Born   1949, Detroit, Michigan

Education and Awards

1967–9	University of Michigan, School of Art, Ann Arbor, Michigan
1972	BFA, Cranbrook Academy of Art, Bloomfield Hills, Michigan
1976	MFA, California College of Arts and Crafts, Oakland, California
1982, 88	National Endowment for the Arts, Visual Arts Fellowship
1983, 84, 87, 93, 99, 2001	Illinois Arts Council, Artists Fellowship Award
1988, 89	Chicago Artists Abroad Grant
1989	Louis Comfort Tiffany Foundation Award
1996	Chicago Artists International Program Grant
2001	The ArtCouncil Grant

Selected Solo Exhibitions / Collaborative Projects

1988	*Anne Wilson/Dann Nardi*, Chicago Cultural Center, Randolph Gallery, Chicago
1991	*New Work,* Roy Boyd Gallery, Chicago
1992	*The Furs (1985–91),* Halsey Gallery, School of the Arts, College of Charleston, South Carolina
1993	*Body into Culture*, Madison Art Center, Madison, Wisconsin
1994	*New Work,* Roy Boyd Gallery, Chicago
1995	*Recent (hand) Work,* Illinois Wesleyan University, School of Art, Bloomington, Illinois
1995	*Imperfect Sutures*, artist book collaboration with Sally Alatalo, Sara Ranchouse Publishing, Chicago
1996	*Mendings,* Roy Boyd Gallery, Chicago (www.royboydgallery.com/)
1996	*An Inquiry about Hair,* Internet web site, Australian National University, Canberra School of Art
1998	*Voices*, REVOLUTION, Detroit (www.revolutn.com/archive/wils/index.html)
1998	*Voices*, REVOLUTION, New York
1998	*Told and Retold*, collaboration with A.B. Forster, CD Project

Selected Solo Exhibitions / **Collaborative Projects** (continued)

1999	*Told and Retold*, collaboration with A.B. Forster, The Museum for Textiles Contemporary Gallery, Toronto (www.museumfortextiles.on.ca/mtcginfo.html)
2000	*Anatomy of Wear*, Museum of Contemporary Art, Chicago
2000	*Hairinquiry*, archived responses, Internet web site (www.artic.edu/~awilso/)
2001	*Edges*, REVOLUTION, Detroit

Selected Group Exhibitions

1989	*14th International Biennial of Tapestry*, Musee Cantonal des Beaux-Arts, Palais de Rumine, Lausanne, Switzerland
1992	*Hair*, John Michael Kohler Arts Center, Sheboygan, Wisconsin
1995	*Fake Nature*, City Gallery at Chastain, Atlanta, Georgia
1995	*Thread Bare*, Southeastern Center for Contemporary Art, Winston-Salem, North Carolina
1995	*Conceptual Textiles: Material Meanings*, John Michael Kohler Arts Center, Sheboygan, Wisconsin
1996	*Art in Chicago 1945–95*, Museum of Contemporary Art, Chicago
1997	*Works on Paper: New Acquisitions*, Museum of Contemporary Art, Chicago
1997	*Art on the Edge of Fashion*, Arizona State University Art Museum, Tempe, Arizona (tour)
1998	*Memorable Histories and Historic Memories*, Bowdoin College Museum of Art, Brunswick, Maine
1998	*Graphic*, Monash University Gallery, Clayton, Australia
1999	*Textures of Memory: The Poetics of Cloth*, Angel Row Gallery, Nottingham, England (tour)
1999	*Stuff*, TBA Exhibition Space, Chicago
2000	*Out of Line: Drawings by Illinois Artists*, Chicago Cultural Center, Chicago
2000	*Remnants of Memory*, Asheville Museum of Art, North Carolina
2001	*Obsession*, University of California San Diego, La Jolla, California

A Chronicle of Days (detail)
1997–8

Works in Public Collections

Museum of Contemporary Art, Chicago

The Art Institute of Chicago

The Metropolitan Museum of Art, New York

Cranbrook Art Museum, Bloomfield Hills, Michigan

Maxine and Stuart Frankel Foundation of Art, Bloomfield Hills, Michigan

The M.H. De Young Memorial Museum, San Francisco

The Illinois Collection of the State of Illinois Center, Chicago

Sandoz Crop Protection Corporation, Chicago

The Smith, Hinchman, and Grylls Architects, Detroit

California Polytechnic State University, San Louis Obispo, California

Selected Publications and Reviews

1988	*American Craft,* February/March, 'Anne Wilson: Urban Furs', essay by Buzz Spector
1989	*Dialogue,* March/April, review by Devon Golden
1992	*Art in America,* February, review by Sue Taylor
1992	*Arts,* February, review by Kathryn Hixson
1993	*Anne Wilson: Body into Culture* (exhibition catalog), Madison Art Center, Madison, Wisconsin, essay by Kathryn Hixson
1993	*Hair* (exhibition catalog), John Michael Kohler Arts Center, Sheboygan, Wisconsin, essay by Alison Ferris
1994	*New Art Examiner,* Summer, review by Laurie Palmer
1994	*ARTFORUM,* May, review by James Yood
1994	*Chicago Reader,* 18 March, review by Fred Camper
1994	*Chicago Tribune,* 11 March, review by David McCracken
1997	*Fiberarts,* September/October, 'Found Objects in Art: Anne Wilson's taxonomy of memories', essay by Lisa Wainwright
1998	*New Art Examiner,* December 1998/January 1999, review by Dennis Alan Nawrocki
1998	*Memorable Histories and Historic Memories* (exhibition catalog), Bowdoin College Museum of Art, Brunswick, Maine, essays by Alison Ferris and Johanna Drucker

Selected Publications and Reviews (continued)

1998	*Anne Wilson, Voices* (exhibition catalog), REVOLUTION, Detroit and New York, essay by Judith Kirshner
1998	*Conceptual Textiles, Material Meanings* (exhibition catalog), John Michael Kohler Arts Center, Sheboygan, Wisconsin, essay by Alison Ferris
1999	*Art in America,* March, review by Eleanor Heartney
1999	*Told and Retold* (exhibition catalog), The Museum for Textiles Contemporary Gallery, Toronto, essays by Jennifer Fisher and Sarah Quinton
1999	*Fiberarts,* Summer, review by Gerry Craig
1999	*The Globe and Mail,* Toronto, 6 May, review by Blake Gopnik
2000	*American Craft,* December/January, review by James Yood
2000	*Make,* London, September–November, review by Jenni Sorkin
2000	*Third Text 53, Winter,* 'Stain: On Cloth, Stigma, and Shame', essay by Jenni Sorkin
2001	*Sculpture,* March, review by Polly Ullrich
2001	*Reinventing Textiles, Volume 2: Gender and Identity,* Winchester, England: Telos Art Publishing, edited by Janis Jefferies, 'Forbidden Touch: Anne Wilson's Cloth', essay by Alison Ferris

Professional

Professor, Department of Fiber and Material Studies, The School of the Art Institute of Chicago

Anne Wilson is represented by Roy Boyd Gallery, Chicago and REVOLUTION, Detroit and New York

Natural Orders, no. 3
1987–8
Fiber, paint
1 x 1m (40 x 40in)

Foreword

Anne Wilson employs conceptual strategies and perceptual responses to blur the boundaries between categories of artistic practice in an original, compelling way. Utilizing human hair and table linens as primary materials and a form of artmaking traditionally associated with domestic labor – that of hand-stitching – Wilson's work poignantly and elegantly evokes private and social rituals. Her engagement with hair and cloth as powerfully evocative materials and as carriers of culturally constructed meaning began more than a decade ago and underlies all of her mature work presented within this monograph. Most recently, as part of an exhibition project for the Museum of Contemporary Art, Chicago, she created a major new large-scale sculpture entitled *Feast* that, while related to earlier explorations with objects taking the familiar forms of pieces of furniture, has stimulated a new set of investigations. Configured as a monumental banquet table, its expansive horizontal surface also evokes a topography that subtly references landscape. While *Feast* represents new territory for Wilson on a conceptual and physical level, the insistent presence of hair and linen within it reveals her ongoing commitment to probing the histories and memories embedded in materials and found objects – issues with which her work has consistently engaged.

Elizabeth A.T. Smith
James W. Alsdorf Chief Curator
Museum of Contemporary Art, Chicago

Second Skins (detail)
1991
Fiber, paint
280 x 220 x 8cm (111 x 87 x 3in)
Karen Johnson Boyd Collection

I CUT MY HAIR:
1992–3
Hair, glass and steel frames
124 x 38 x 2.5cm
(49 x 15 x 1in) each
Jane Wenger Collection

Blonde and Black
Braided
Raven Waves
Crimson Dyed

Postminimal and After

I: General Terms: History and Skin

"Between the abstract and the meadow
  hurls the chaos.
Between the Diaspora and the crinoline sits
  the poem."

Bonnie Sherk, *High Performance* magazine,
1980

Anne Wilson belongs, in terms of loyalty
and education, to the current long moment
of postminimalism. In this moment,
hierarchies that had organized and driven
both art history and popular culture for over
a century have come unhinged. They flap
and bang in that same wind from Paradise
that has dumped the vast wreck of the past
at the feet of Walter Benjamin's "Angel of
History". This last decade of Wilson's work
compiles into a sort of epic narrative, full of
domestic incident and charged with a
sexuality that dissolves into abstraction.

This mutual dissolution between the abstract
and the erotic is something that Eva Hesse
remarks about Claes Oldenburg in her
notebooks (undated, circa 1967), and that
critics of the seventies identified as Hesse's
own central, or essential, contradiction. The
terms they coined to convey this
contradiction, like "serial surrealism," apply
as well to Wilson, whose work commands a
reading that is at once academically formalist
and intimately anecdotal; a reading that

Hair Work
1991–3
Hair, thread, cloth
161 x 140 x 9cm (63.5 x 55.5 x 3.5in)
Museum of Contemporary Art, Chicago

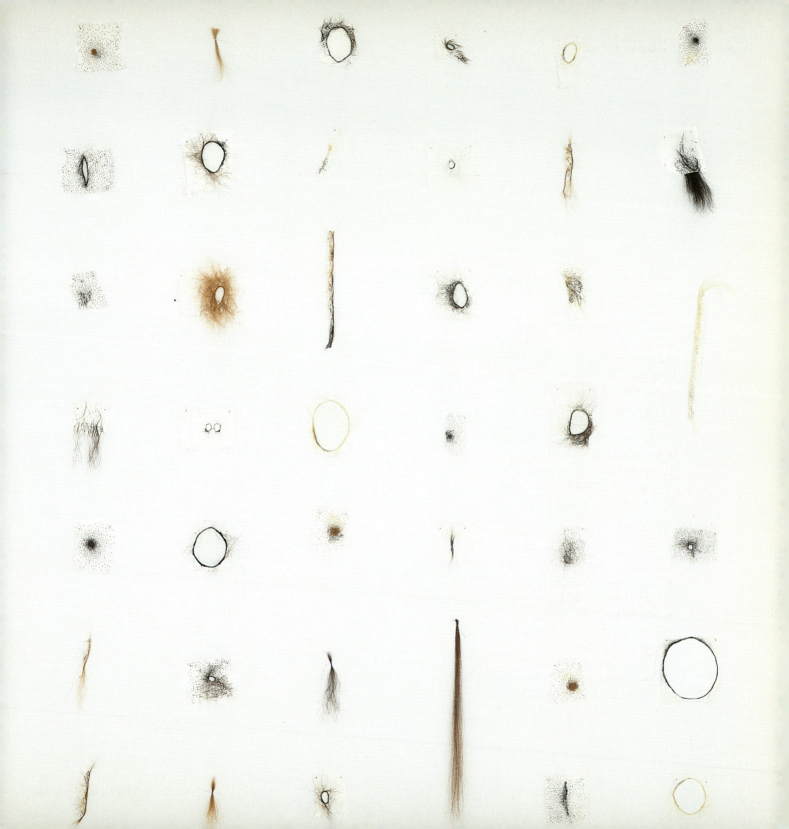

Second Skins (detail)
1991

constantly interrupts itself and goes in
circles. And, postmodern or not, the story
the critic ends up telling is less about
influence than about discipleship. Just as
Hesse's trajectory can be described as a
departure from and return to the Sublime, as
personified by Agnes Martin, so Wilson's
trajectory begins with Hesse's late work, and
moves forward from there.

Both Hesse and Oldenburg, and many
artists of the Art Fabric movement, explored
the soft and fugitive qualities of textile
materials in work that, by standing between
abstraction and depiction, placed itself as
well between mind and body, in the
intercessionary space Henri Bergson
assigns to memory. Artwork that intercedes
between mind and body, between (in Alan
Kaprow's terms) art-about-art and art-
about-life, will inevitably seek those
reconciliations in the past. For some artists
who specifically reference childhood, the
past is personal, while for others it is a more
complex mix of the personal and the social.
Their intercessions take place both within
the artworld and without, where political
and family issues are resolved. Whether
they are healers like Donna Henes, or
politicians like Joseph Beuys, their work
tends towards an often trivialized nostalgia,
a profound sadness.

Mourning Cloth (drape)
1992–3
Hair, thread, reconstructed cloth
183 x 81 x 5cm (72 x 32 x 2in)

The San Francisco Bay Area Feminism from which Wilson emerged in the seventies, took this sadness, and the general cultural contempt for the feminine, as its navigational poles; its points of departure. This is the situation that Bonnie Sherk summed up as "between the Diaspora and the crinoline." This is where Wilson, like so many of her contemporaries (Rachel Whiteread, Ann Hamilton, Annette Messager, Tim Hawkinson) finds both her "found objects" and her foundational subject. It is where we enter the space of the body and the social unconscious of its memory, through the warm imprint of its clothing and the history of its skin.

The skin is where we find ourselves; its history is ours. Our Vitruvian Man is an inflatable bag, a rubber sheet, a mattress, a scrap of table-linen. These are both the familiar objects and the uncanny subject of recent art. Forty years ago, Rauschenberg had to apologize to the general public for using a family quilt in a painting (Bed, 1955). He made up an elaborate lie about how poverty had driven him to do something that now seems natural and obvious. That which was "surreal" in Hesse's work has now yielded its superfluous prefix, and become, simply, real.

Lost (detail)
1998

Mourning Cloth (drape - detail)
1992–3
Hair, thread, reconstructed cloth
183 x 81 x 5cm (72 x 32 x 2in)

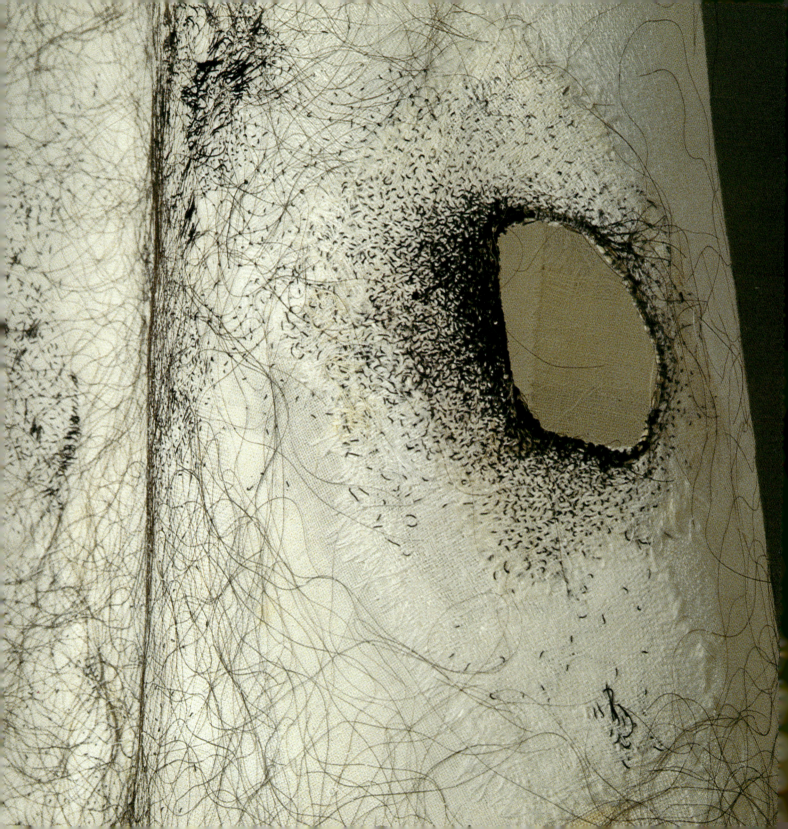

Grafts (#1)
1993
Hair, thread, cloth
104 x 99 x 6cm (41 x 39 x 2.5in)
Tom Talucci Collection

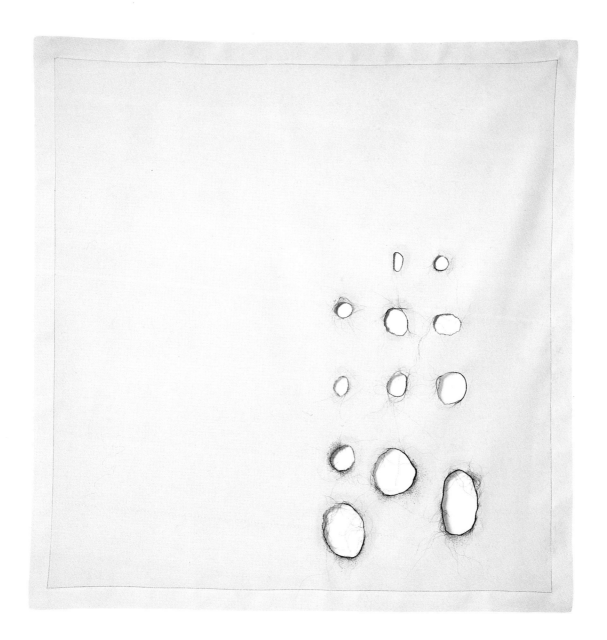

Grafts (#2)
1993
Hair, thread, cloth
127 x 124 x 7cm (50 x 49 x 2.5in)
Museum of Contemporary Art, Chicago

II: Specifics: Linen, Hair, the Closet and the Table

Hair comes and goes from our lives, erupting and fading in ways that embarrass us, always. Our hair tells us that we are getting old, that we could use a bath, a trip to the barber or the beautician; that we need to pay attention to what is happening. The accumulation of thousands of early-morning sessions at the mirror, reading the morning's memos from our bodies (this is your hair, it's turning white, it's falling out, it's growing from your nose and ears and that odd mole on your forehead, so much like your mother's, pay attention) becomes a paradigm for all of our discoveries of inattention; for remembering. There is an obvious logic to the Victorian lockets with twists of hair in them, a logic that extends from this daily experience of forgetting and remembering. Samuel Beckett writes, in his meditation on Proust, that the man with a really good memory never remembers anything because he never forgot it in the first place. Hair, beginning with your own hair, presents you with your most frequent reminders that you are not that perfect man.

Anne Wilson's three major works from 1998, *Lost, Misplaced* and *Found* all speak to this engagement that hair has with remembering in its everyday dance with forgetting. The hair in *Lost* has some of the same comical displacement and dreamlike condensation that the fat has in Joseph Beuys' *Fat Chair* from 1963. And though every single hair is delicately couched in place, as a whole they appear to form an unruly mass, a mat, a wilderness. What is lost here is presumably the (hairy, male) body for whom this shroud was made, and the surprising efflorescence of hair, absolutely dense at its limit, reminds us what a surprise death is, and what a joke. The body becomes its dress and vanishes, the oldest piece of magic we know, leaving its hair behind as a guidepost to fear and desire.

These folds have an elegant, imperial simplicity. They remind us of the simple dress that came at the beginning and end of Victorian excess, and also of the smocks worn traditionally by little girls, artists and clowns. Their drape is all about gravity, but is still a possible vehicle for low comedy. The reading we give them derives from both public and private history: shared facts and family secrets.

"If we give objects the friendship they should have, we do not open a wardrobe without a slight start. Beneath its russet wood, a wardrobe is a very white almond. To open it, is to experience an event of whiteness."
Gaston Bachelard, *The Poetics of Space*, 1958

Devour

1993

Hair, thread, cloth

94 x 95 x 10cm

(37 x 37.5 x 2in)

Museum of Contemporary Art, Chicago

And the hair that Wilson stitches to the surface of this cloth recalls the lives that come and go in the family that curates both the cloth and the memory of its provenance. The damask, under its film of hair, records the collision of specific, lost bodies and a recuperated family history. The family's history is its secret, put away and recovered, time and again. But the intimate loss that the hair records, in a huge, painstaking labor, as each hair is stitched in place and out of the damask a skin is made, is universal.

This collision between the familiarly social and the universally intimate is present throughout the decade of work that this monograph records. Back in 1991, Wilson had just finished a cycle of faux cowhides, made of synthetic felt and various fibers, natural and acrylic, painted and then stitched together. The edge between the natural and the artificial had become unproductive for her, and she was looking for materials and contexts with more social and personal resonance. After all, the intuition that science (and art) is socially constructed only returns us to the social, which then demands, like the hair on the toothbrush, that we pay attention.

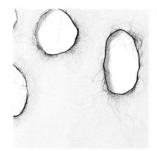

Grafts (#2) (detail)
1993

A Chronicle of Days [10.25.97–1.20.98]
1997–8
Hair, thread, cloth
183 x 587cm (72 x 231in)

Her attention drew her first to hair as a social institution, as a trade. The falls of commercial hair that we see in *I CUT MY HAIR* (1992–3), are the early works in this cycle – a false start in a way, in that it worked too well, too soon. Framing the falls between glass and presenting them in pairs was simple and direct, and exhausted itself as a first impulse. But the hair remained present in her studio, as did an inheritance of linen, much of which was worn beyond use. Sometimes an artist's studio is like a dream in which condensations of meaning and material follow their own logic. The first result of this encounter was *Hair Work* (1991–3), a grid of possible variations on the combination of hair and linen, and out of these variations came the "disrepairs," the mends and holes, edgings and resurfacings, glazings and furrings that make up the balance of Wilson's work of the last ten years.

"Why make a hole? Too big for a button. This is about letting something through, not preparing the way for another type of closure. Wilson has elaborated on imperfection: a patch of wear, a rip in the tablecloth."
Laurie Palmer, *New Art Examiner*, 1994

Where the linen is burned, stained or worn threadbare, Wilson fills or amends its rupture with human hair. Where the hole is too large to be bridged over, she binds its edges and disrepairs it, curates it, making it suddenly shockingly human and intimate. Where the weave is continuous but worn, the disrepair consists of blots of stitched hair that raise the surface into warty little islands of stubble. She then gathers these anonymous personifications into suites of labor, first *Areas of Disrepair* (1993–8), and then *A Chronicle of Days* (1997–8) and *Feast* (2000).

The sense her process supplies of a life measured out in regular increments of self-imposed labor led her, in *A Chronicle of Days*, to return to the grid of *Hair Work*. Here, the grid records one hundred days between July 1997 and February 1998. Here the scraps vary from deluxe damask to humble dishtowel, though mostly the former, and the "tangles, snarls, knots, wads, webs, blurs, smudges, nicks, snags, snares, splats, puckers, bursts, blobs or floaters," (Judith Kirshner, *Anne Wilson, Voices,* catalog, 1998) vary in size, density and location. Framed in sequence, in a massive two- by six-meter (six- by nineteen-foot) collectivity, they evoke nothing so much as one of Larry Poons' musical/metrical dot paintings, as each disrepair rises or falls, grows or shrinks relative to its neighbor, next frame over.

Lost
1998
Hair, thread, cloth, leather cord, wood chair
91 x 56 x 60cm (36 x 22 x 23.5in)

It seems that everyone who responds to
Wilson's work does so in terms of personal
memories of hair, as something found and
lost. So, to accompany the premiére
exhibition of the *Chronicle* (at
REVOLUTION, in Detroit), she presented a
sound installation (executed in collaboration
with multi-media artist A.B. Forster) of
personal narratives about hair, *Told and
Retold*. These were selected from two years
of responses to Wilson's interactive website,
An Inquiry about Hair (www.artic.edu/
~awilso/). On her site, she asks how it feels
to lose your hair, and what it means to cut
your hair. Each of the headsets gridded into
a kind of chorus on the gallery wall contains
a single answer.

Like the grand finale of a fireworks display,
this decade of work concludes with a heroic
coda, aptly entitled *Feast*. Here, all of
Wilson's motifs of hair work (holes, dots,
splotches and edges), in all of the colors in
which hair is found, are gathered together
atop a seven-meter (twenty-two-foot) table.
Each linen fragment is fixed to the tabletop
with mapping pins, and the cumulative
object evokes a *Wunderkammer* fantasy, in
which a map of the moon is pinned together
from a collection of exotic plants and
insects, or a parade-ground tableau in
which the senior class forms itself into the
image of the national flag. Though each tiny

actor is irreducibly individual, what they are
doing, looping through memory, is acting
out an abstraction.

The resolution this points to (we are not
there yet, though we are going there) is one
in which the oppositions that characterize
postminimalism (Diaspora and crinoline;
abstraction and meadow) are sublimated,
transcended and left behind. But we are not
there, yet. We are taking the scenic route.

Tim Porges
Writer, critic, and art librarian; former Editor,
White Walls magazine

Found
1998
Hair, thread, cloth
267 x 66 x 25cm (105 x 26 x 10in)
The Art Institute of Chicago

Told and Retold:
an inquiry about hair
1998
Anne Wilson in collaboration
with A.B. Forster
Sound installation: audio
cassettes, head sets, cables,
cloth, wood

Told and Retold:
an inquiry about hair
(detail of one listener)
1998
Anne Wilson in collaboration
with A.B. Forster
Sound installation: audio cassettes,
head sets, cables, cloth, wood

Feast

History is embedded in these white remnants. At once recalling an imagined past and breathing into them a prolonged life. Glistening slivers of fabric stall traces of passing time. Used and used and used until they tore. Surgical incisions are carved with wear. Handled by generations, these threads are inherited.

Refined dining atelier, instituting cleanliness of mind, body and behaviour. This linen is not sanctified as a voice of the bourgeoisie. This linen leads you astray.

Hair appears on these crisp surfaces like cracks in the face of polite society. Raised thornless roses deprived of their colour are not to be marked with something else. How provocatively *Feast* casts a glance of disdain on propriety. How subversively *Feast* adopts the sensuality of hair. Tumbling locks are turned into stitched mendings, bruises and wounds are cradled. And how with indignation the cloth is liberated from its innate politeness, of a hitherto resignation to a woven role. This fabric of life screams to assert equilibrium.

Feast
2000
Hair, thread, cloth, pins, wood table
80 x 168 x 671cm (31.5 x 66 x 264in)
Museum of Contemporary Art, Chicago

Domestic rites attached to family dining, cooking, and cleaning are returned to in thought, as are the meals themselves, revolving around this linen. Behind closed doors what might have been said, what rules laid down, surprises hurled?

No matter what morsel falls upon white sanctity, it can and will be washed; bleached out, no residue of disruption. Damask must be washed and pressed each time it is used, a single stain will ruin it.

Such exquisite shadows concede to mortality and claim familial lineage in memory. As clothes bear the mark of their owner even when he or she no longer appears. Magic is invested in cloth and clothes. Wear an item of clothing to be close to someone gone. Cloth on skin. An anonymous pile of clothing left on the floor. Who wore them before they were left?

Do you know what lover or enemy ate the last meal which adorned this table cloth? This inanimate witness. Absent lives revolt against entangling decorum.

Scraps of food fell, lay bereft uneaten. Knives scratched china and in their shine seized their surroundings. A single strand of hair left a scalp. A surrogate for the self or another. Dropped to the cloth, its new home amidst appetites for *Feast*. Does *Feast* perhaps inspire a taste for the body, or disgust? Hair protrudes from these cloths as truth sprouts from the skin of masquerade.

The table is cleared and the cloth burns with the outcast dread of disgust. Frays in hands and turns to pieces. Clusters of cells divide. Disperse, matter recoils, hollows form to mark the zone of dissension. Take a needle sharp enough to draw blood. Blood, red as the bleached roses once were.

Damage is preserved. Stitches which clasp together wounded flesh are abhorrent here. The rips, the tears, the holes, they honour imperfection. These extant breaches are cared for with human fibre, conserving every blemish. With every stitch that binds a strand, voids and tears are nurtured. Alchemy prepares them. Desire for sedition is met. Don't patch, fill, restore or defend

Feast (detail)
2000
Hair, thread, cloth, pins, wood table
80 x 168 x 671cm (31.5 x 66 x 264in)

Feast (detail)
2000

the void. Keep it, see it, explore it. This worn away signature of reality. Corporeality is imposed. Motifs of insurgent duplicity. A sublime collision of body and veneer, speaking to and from realms which are rarely given the chance to draw breath, let alone articulate that which is not subsumed by easy harmony.

The weave of the cloth is controlled; inch by inch is taut. Hair is unrestrained. Stray tangled lines crawl into volcanic nestlings. Tidy black mounds tighten until they rise puckered. Slits, garnering lengths of hair for protection, expel the immaculate vastness beyond. Slashes are the cloth's supportive ageing spine. A confession of traction is irremovable. Releasing tales found in the folds of the linen. Remembrance in cloth lingers like an afterthought. This great *Feast*, this surplus of the unsaid.

Myth adheres to matter and arouses a return, fools minds, jolts them into recall. This insignia of hair on cloth taunts and dares hidden fears. Here is the utmost deliverance of the border between the precious and the grotesque. Stitches found in exile. Such refinement being defied . . . yet not; strangely pleasing to those fragments of cloth on this great white table.

Feast is a legacy which implicates the present. Identity is claimed and withdrawn; the hair belonged to someone. To whom and when is both a mystery asking to be told and an irrelevance. Hair without bodies proposes loss. Where are the origins of this hair? Lives are evoked through matter separated from them. We groom the deceased stuff on our heads, treat it as beloved cargo with a heartbeat of its own. Does hair without a body provoke a confrontation with human mortality, with the mortality of seamlessness? Does the hair phobic rile in confrontation with separated hair because of its thundering intimate polemic?

An implausible simultaneity, the absence and presence of unknown bodies. Intimacies brought forth and in some sense negated. Like bits of food one wants to remove, like stains that cannot be washed out, distraction has become resident, fixed, stitch after stitch, mended into the material.

Absence is corroborated by DNA; the accomplice of truant bodies. Flesh is known without being known. Locks of hair in Victorian jewelled lockets, photographs, and DNA memorise a body, lost, missing, temporally displaced. They are proxy for a definite presence. One thread of hair, and there is presence again. Visibility is coded into an eyelash, a nail clipping, a strand of hair. A record of the body even when it is not there. Even when it is not complete. Is the disappearance of the whole and the presence of a part haunting you?

Sate a hunger for a way around – or a way into – the body. In a forensic expedition *Feast* traverses the body with a simmering haste. *Feast* is a map. A map of fossil flesh and warm insides, as well as not so ancient ruins or singed vestiges. Internal and external edges of the body are perforated. Inside and out, they morph, become one plotted domain. The dual territories of this landscape are equivocally staked.

Look down upon *Feast* from a height and meet a volatile universe. Lower your eyes to brave the edge of *Feast*, and navigate your way through gatherings of cells, pass these membranes of hair which protect the torn, safely bound by pins. Stand on the periphery and behold outskirts in your eyes. A sudden darkness is found, brocades of hair pursue marred curves. A cobweb of the body, the finest lines, threads, strands, meshed. Generic configurations – perhaps some yearn to wander – settle with familiar stock.

Red speckled stitches are dense then sparse, flecks feed into *Feast*. Tiny cavities, embraced by the cold metal of long insect pins clutch *Feast*. Straggling hairs line these cells, these minuscule ruptures. Detached locks of hair are frozen, pinned so that they may not escape in a tryst of indemnity. *Feast*'s eruptions mimic lines of the body, a slope here and a hollow there, pursuing a proposition of bodily material.

The material memory connives with imaginings, conjuring worlds which loot past associations and inscribe new scenarios. I imagine two figures clothed in dark suits, their imposition lightened only by starched white shirts, presiding at the head of this table. This topography of hair is their imagined fear. Repression unleashed, protocol sabotaged – there could not be hair at this table. It is pinned down, they cannot remove it. Their horror is exaggerated by the length of the table. And when this emperor and empress of sustenance vanish in my mind, the hair is not just angry or defiant. It summons lives past with a similar kind of respect accorded to relics. It is not simply abject or horrific, it is elegant, eloquently raging, with disquieting grace. Without aggression, without the pain of attack. It is a rightful catharsis of past and present.

Hattie Gordon

Freelance writer and critic; Marjorie Susman Curatorial Fellow (2000) and curator of *Anne Wilson: Anatomy of Wear* at the Museum of Contemporary Art, Chicago

Other titles in this series

Vol 3: Caroline Broadhead (UK)
by Jeremy Theophilus
Shadows, windows, invisibility...
examine some of the inspirational
threads animating Britain's winner of
the Jerwood Prize for Textiles.
ISBN 1902015231

Vol 4: Chika Ohgi (Japan)
by Keiko Kawashima
Be enchanted by one of Kyoto's finest
artists working in installations with paper.
She composes her work using space itself
as an equal presence.
ISBN 1902015258

Vol 5: Anne Marie Power (Australia)
by Dr Juliette Peers
Textile artist, papermaker and sculptor,
Power plays upon the issues of cultural
trafficking and influences between
continent and continent.
ISBN 1902015266

Vol 6: Anne Wilson (USA)
by Tim Porges and Hattie Gordon
This important American artist uses human
hair, table linens and hand-stitching to probe
poignant personal memories and histories,
as well as evoking a subtle sense of landscape.
ISBN 1902015223

Vol 7: Alice Kettle (UK)
by Dr Jennifer Harris
up close and intimate with probably
largest machine embroideries in the world
dating from 1997–2002, including a move
landscape.
1902015312

Vol 8: Helen Lancaster (Australia)
by Carolyn Skinner
The perilous fragility of nature, beautifully depicted
by an outstanding conceptual environmentalist using
embroidery and fabric manipulation.
ISBN 1902015290

Vol 9: Kay Lawrence (Australia)
by Dr Diana Wood Conroy
One of the world's top tapestry weavers, her recent
work negotiates issues about identity in textures
ranging from minimal to lush, from sensuous to spiky.
ISBN 1902015282

Vol 10: Joan Livingstone (USA)
by Gerry Craig
Livingstone's powerful installations incorporate felt,
stitch and epoxy resin. Professor of Fiber and Material
Studies at the School of the Art Institute, Chicago, she
is one of America's most important fiber sculptors.
ISBN 1902015274

Vol 11: Marian Smit (Netherlands)
by Marjolein v.d. Stoep
1st Prize winner in Third International Paper Triennal,
Switzerland, 1999. "Work of great simplicity
combining technique and poetry."
ISBN 1902015320

Vol 12: Chiyoko Tanaka (Japan)
by Lesley Millar
Tanaka's prized weavings are in public collections
around the world. A leading light from Kyoto,
her work is breathtaking and awe-inspiring.
ISBN 190201524X

still available:

Vol 1: Jilly Edwards (UK)
by Lene Bragger and Melanie Cook
ISBN 1902015207

Vol 2: Marian Bijlenga (Netherlands)
by Jack Lenor Larsen and Gert Staal
ISBN 1902015215

visit **www.arttextiles.com to order any of our titles
online or to view a list of our international stockists**